MY LIFE AS A

MUSLIM

FLEUR BRADLEY

45TH PARALLEL PRESS

Published in the United States of America by Cherry Lake Publishing Group
Ann Arbor, Michigan
www.cherrylakepublishing.com

Editorial Consultant: Dr. Virginia Loh-Hagan, EdD, Literacy, San Diego State University
Content Adviser: Molly H. Bassett, Associate Professor and Chair in the Department of Religious Studies
    at Georgia State University
Reading Adviser: Beth Walker Gambro, MS, Ed., Reading Consultant, Yorkville, IL
Book Designer: Jen Wahi

Photo Credits: © Leysan/istock, cover, 1; © KiyechkaSo/Shutterstock, 4; © Ebtikar/Shutterstock, 8; Public Domain/
    Wikimedia, 11; © The Walters Art Museum/Acquired by Henry Walters/Created by Shaykh ʿAbbasi/Acc. No.
    W.668.10B, 12; © Oakland Images/Shutterstock, 14; © Aisylu Ahmadieva/Shutterstock, 17; © Source Andrzej
    Kłossowski/Wikimedia, 19; © nelen/Shutterstock, 20; © TonyV3112/Shutterstock, 24; © Rawpixel.com/
    Shutterstock, 27; © Zull Must/Shutterstock, 28; © munir sukamoto/Shutterstock, 29; © sokolander/Shutterstock, 30

45th Parallel Press is an imprint of Cherry Lake Publishing Group.

Library of Congress Cataloging-in-Publication Data

Names: Bradley, Fleur, author.
Title: My life as a Muslim / by Fleur Bradley.
Description: Ann Arbor : Cherry Lake Publishing, 2022. | Series: How the world worships
Identifiers: LCCN 2021039875 | ISBN 9781534199422 (hardcover) | ISBN 9781668900567 (paperback) |
    ISBN 9781668906323 (ebook) | ISBN 9781668902004 (pdf)
Subjects: LCSH: Islam—Juvenile literature. | Islam—Essence, genius, nature—Juvenile literature.
Classification: LCC BP161.3 .B7135 2022 | DDC 297—dc23
LC record available at https://lccn.loc.gov/2021039875

Printed in the United States of America
Corporate Graphics

ABOUT THE AUTHOR:

Fleur Bradley is originally from the Netherlands. She likes to travel and learn about different cultures whenever she can. Fleur has written many stories for kids and educational books. She now lives in Colorado with her family.

TABLE OF CONTENTS

Introduction

Religions are systems of faith and worship. Do you practice a religion? About 80 percent of the world's population does. That's 4 out of 5 people.

Every religion is different. Some have one God. That's called **monotheism**. Other religions have multiple gods. This is called **polytheism**. Some religions have an **icon** instead of a god. An icon is an important figure. Islam is a monotheistic religion.

Islam is the world's second largest religion. About 24 percent of people in the world are Muslim. In the United States, only about 1 percent of people are Muslim. Most Muslims live in Asian nations near the western Pacific Ocean. Large populations of Muslims live in Bangladesh, Indonesia, India, Iran, Pakistan, and Turkey.

Muslims believe in one God. They believe Muhammad was the final prophet. A prophet is a messenger of God. Muhammad went to the Cave of Hira. This is in Saudi Arabia. He was 40 years old. He meditated. Meditate means to clear your mind of all thoughts.

Muhammad heard the voice of an angel. The voice was of Jibrail, or Gabriel. The angel told him to "Proclaim! Proclaim in the name of your Lord who created!" Jibrail went on to tell Muhammad he had to recite the words. They are now part of the **Qur'an**. The Qur'an is Islam's holy book.

Muhammad continued to receive revelations from Jibrail. Revelations are secret things that are made known. These are also part of the Qur'an. Not everyone liked Muhammad's teachings. He ran away with his followers. They went to Medina.

Another important religious text is the **Sunna**. The Sunna includes Muhammad's words and deeds.

Islam has different branches. This includes the **Sunni**, **Shi'a**, and the **Sufi**. Each has a different belief on who can be a leader. A leader in Islam is called a **caliph**. The Sunni believe caliphs should be elected by Muslims. Shi'a believe leadership should come from **descendants** of Muhammad. A descendant is someone who is related to a person in the past. The Sufi believe Islam should focus on spiritual growth over wealth and power.

Islam values peace and knowledge. It had a Golden Age from 750 to 1258 CE. That was when Muslim scientists, artists, and philosophers made major changes to the world. For example, Muslim doctors created some of the first medical schools.

MECCA AND PRAYER

The prophet Muhammad was born in Mecca in current-day Saudi Arabia. Mecca is an important city for Muslims. Islam expects followers to make the pilgrimage to Mecca at least once in their life.

Muslims pray 5 times a day, in the direction of Mecca. It is called Salah.

Prayer must be done:

1. Between first daylight and sunrise

2. Right after midday

3. Mid-afternoon

4. After sunset, but before it's dark

5. When it's dark

Muslims must be clean at the time of prayer. Prayer is often done on a prayer mat.

Yasir
American Muslim

CHAPTER 1
AN AMERICAN MUSLIM

"You need to eat, Asim," I tell my little brother. "It's a long day still." Today is the last day of Ramadan. Ramadan is the celebration of Muhammad hearing Allah's wisdom. Allah means God in Arabic. Ramadan lasts about a month.

During Ramadan I fast throughout the day. I get up when it's still dark to have breakfast. I'm too tired to eat. But I do. It's the only time I can eat until after sunset. During Ramadan we don't eat between sunrise and sunset. It's hard, because I have a bunch of tests at school. By the end of the day, I'm always starving!

Asim nods and stretches. "Tomorrow is **Eid al-Fitr**," he says with a smile. Eid al-Fitr is the celebration of the end of Ramadan. *"Finally,"* he adds before shoving in another bite.

I nod my head. "Yes, finally." We are not supposed to be impatient. But Ramadan can feel long. I'm one of the few Muslims at school. Sometimes it's hard seeing everyone else eat.

"Let's wash up," I tell Asim. We wash our faces, hands, and forearms to prepare to pray. This is called **wudu**.

Yasir talks about being one of the few
Muslims in his school. His classmates don't
always understand Ramadan. There are
other religions that have fasting as a ritual,
however. Can you find examples?

Asim splashes me with water. I laugh and splash him back.

"Settle down," our mother says as she passes. "You need to hurry with prayer. Otherwise, you'll miss your bus."

Asim and I dry off and go to our living room. There, we have prayer mats set up. We bow, kneel, and touch our foreheads to the ground to pray.

After prayer, Asim and I get ready for school. It's going to be a long day. But I'm excited for tomorrow!

At school, I sit with my friend Alex at lunch. It's hard to watch him unpack his food, so I look away. Plus, he eats bologna, which has pork in it. As a Muslim, I'm only allowed to eat **halal food**. This is food permitted by the Qur'an.

"Sorry, Yasir," he says. Alex eats quickly, then asks, "Ramadan ends this evening, right?"

Did you know? Muslims believe in many prophets.

I nod as I take out my notes. I have a math quiz later and need to review.

"What's it really for, Ramadan?" Alex asks. We've been friends since first grade. He has no religion but is always interested to hear about Islam. My religion is a big part of my life.

Math will need to wait. I love talking about my religion. "It's to remember Muhammad's revelation from Allah," I say.

Did you know? Mary, the mother of Jesus, is mentioned in the Qur'an. She's the only woman named in the holy book.

JIHAD

Jihad is an important ideal in Islam. It means "striving" or "struggling" in Arabic. Jihad means living in the way of Allah. It means living in a positive and peaceful way.

The term is sometimes used in a negative way to reference military holy war. But to most Muslims, jihad means living according to Muslim rules. Jihad means doing this even when it's difficult.

I think about this during Ramadan. "Also, it reminds me to be thankful for all that I have."

Alex nods and puts away his lunch box. "So, what are you going to do tomorrow? Eat for hours?"

We laugh.

I say, "Pretty much. My mom is cooking up a storm."

Alex smiles. "You know that's going to be good." He's been over to my house a lot and loves her cooking.

"Tell you what," I say. "I'll save you some baklava."

Did you know? Muslims invented coffee during the 1400s.

CHAPTER 2
CELEBRATING EID AL-FITR

I wake up on Eid al-Fitr, looking forward to the day ahead. Asim jumps up out of bed when I go to wake him.

"*Eid Mubarak*," I whisper. It means "Blessed be your celebration."

"It's Eid!" Asim calls.

Our father passes his bedroom. "Indeed, it is. Let's get ready for the day!"

Our parents asked the school for the day off. For my cousins in New York City, Eid is a holiday. But not here in Arizona. We'll miss a day of school. Not that I mind too much!

We put on our best clothes. Even Asim does and he usually doesn't bother. Once everyone is ready, we drive to the **mosque**. A mosque is a place where Muslims worship.

The mosque is full. We first say hello to my uncle, aunt, and cousins. Our family has already made a **Zakat ul-Fitr**. That's giving to charity. We do this to help the poor. It is a custom around Ramadan.

We go inside the mosque. We take off our shoes and wash.

We pray. Then there is a sermon by our **imam**. An imam is a Muslim leader and teacher. We ask for Allah's forgiveness, as well as peace and blessings for all.

Our grandparents are buried in the cemetery. After the sermon, the men in our family pay their respects.

Is there a mosque in your area? What services and celebrations are held there?

Then it's time to celebrate! Our mosque has a community center where we all get together. Everyone brings their favorite dish. There are curries, fruits, and dates. Mom made her amazing baklava.

All the kids get gifts. Asim got a kite. I got more paint for my art.

HOLIDAYS

Muslims follow a lunar calendar. Lunar means moon. The calendar Muslims follow relies on the moon cycle to determine holidays. Here are some holidays a Muslim might observe:

Al-Hijra: The first day of Muharram, which is the first month of the Islamic year. It celebrates when Muhammad moved from Mecca to Medina.

Ashura: Takes place on tenth day of Muharram. It celebrates Islamic martyrs who died for Islam.

Ramadan: The ninth month of the Islamic year. It's a month of fasting that commemorates when Allah revealed his wisdom to Muhammad.

Eid al-Fitr: During the first 3 days of Shawwal, the tenth month of the Islamic calendar. It celebrates the end of Ramadan and fasting.

Eid al-Adha: Called the Festival of Sacrifice, it takes place on the tenth day of Dhu al-Hijja. That is the twelfth month in the Islamic year. It celebrates the prophet Abraham and his sacrifices for Islam.

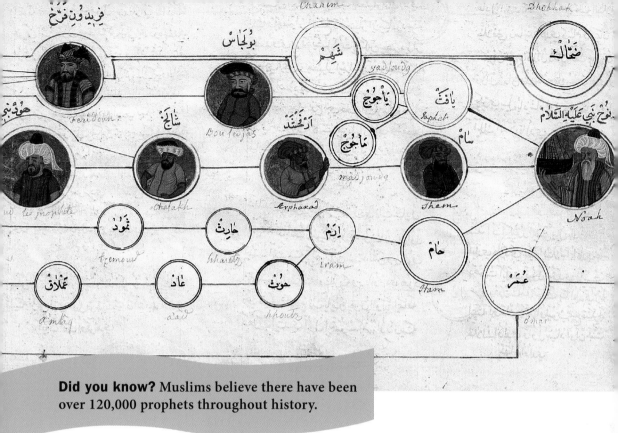

Did you know? Muslims believe there have been over 120,000 prophets throughout history.

There is music and games. People exchange Eid cards. My cousin Sabina paints girls' hands with pretty designs using henna. Henna is a colored paste that temporarily colors your skin.

"Do you think we can take it out?" Asim asks me, waving his kite. "There's the park across the street," he adds.

"In a minute," I say. "I'm still working on my food." I have a plate piled high with sweets. Eid al-Fitr comes only once a year, after all!

Badia
Pakistani Muslim

CHAPTER 3
A YOUNG MUSLIM ON A PILGRIMAGE

"How much longer until we're there?" my twin sister Faiza asks. We're on our spiritual hajj. This means we're traveling to Mecca. Mecca is in the mountains of Saudi Arabia. Only Muslims can enter during hajj. This is because Mecca is a holy city. Clearly Faiza is more impatient. I, on the other hand, am enjoying this trip. It's one I may never make again! We live in Pakistan. So the trip is pretty long. The trip takes over 7 hours—even when we travel by plane!

Father says, "No complaining, Faiza. We're almost there anyway." He seems nervous, as does our mother. Hajj is important for Muslims. Hajj is the Fifth Pillar of Islam. The Five Pillars are things we should do as Muslims to live a good life.

We have been looking forward to this trip. All 4 of us are dressed in white robes and dresses.

Our family enters the mountains through 1 of the 4 gaps. My feet are sore, but I don't complain.

SIX ARTICLES OF FAITH

According to the Six Articles of Faith, Muslims must believe in:

1. One God

2. God's angels

3. The book of Qur'an

4. God's prophets, especially Muhammad

5. Judgment Day

6. God's supreme will

Mecca is a big, busy city. Because hajj is the annual pilgrimage happening now, it's very crowded. Our mother said that there are millions of Muslims who travel here every year!

We reach the Ka'ba, a cube-shaped building in the center of Mecca. I grab Faiza's hand, even though it's July and very hot. The city is so busy that it scares me a little.

"It's okay, Badia," Faiza says to reassure me.

Mother guides us along. "Stay with me, girls."

It is tradition for pilgrims to kiss the sacred Black Stone. I feel very nervous, like everyone is watching me. We must hurry along. There are millions more here to perform the rituals of hajj.

We then walk around the Ka'ba 7 more times, counter-clockwise. This is called **tawaf**. I feel light-headed from the heat and the importance of the moment.

I also feel lifted by all the Muslims around me. I feel especially close to Allah and the prophet Muhammad.

"Are you ready to go to the Great Mosque?" Mother asks us.

Both Faiza and I nod. It's an honor to be here. Plus, we're ready to get out of the hot sun!

All Muslims are required to make a pilgrimage to Mecca. Look up Mecca. If you had to travel there, what would this journey look like for you? How is it different from Badia and her family? How is it the same?

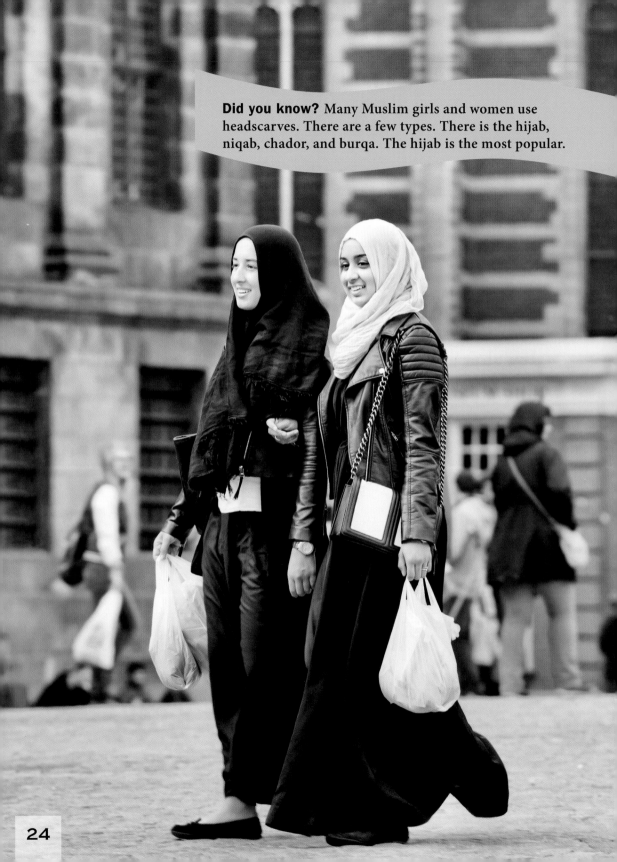

Did you know? Many Muslim girls and women use headscarves. There are a few types. There is the hijab, niqab, chador, and burqa. The hijab is the most popular.

CHAPTER 4
MECCA CELEBRATIONS

We have our service in the Great Mosque in Mecca. I try to pay attention as much as possible. This is a once-in-a-lifetime trip.

Faiza is impatient. I can feel her wiggle beside me during prayer.

Finally, we go to our hotel in Mecca. We're fortunate. Some have to stay in tents outside Mecca because it's too crowded.

After many more rituals to honor Islam, it is Eid al-Adha. It marks the end of hajj. Eid al-Adha celebrates the sacrifices the prophet Abraham made for Islam. It's also when the Feast of Sacrifice begins.

THE FIVE PILLARS

The Qur'an discusses Five Pillars of Faith. These are duties a Muslim must follow to live a good life.

Shahadah: Muslims must make a statement of faith. This is done by saying "There is no god but God, and Muhammad is his prophet."

Salah or Salat: Muslims must pray at set times, 5 times a day.

Zakat or Zakah: Muslims have the duty to give to the needy or poor.

Sawm: Muslims must fast during Ramadan. Ramadan is the holy month in Islam where Muslims fast and reflect on their religion.

Hajj: Muslims must make the pilgrimage to Mecca.

Men slaughter, or kill, sheep and goats. It sounds a little scary, but we give the meat to the poor.

"I don't think I can ever eat meat again," Faiza says afterward. We're back at our hotel.

I laugh and nod. "That was something," I say. It's been a busy 5 days of hajj.

Did you know? Masjid al-Haram is considered the most sacred mosque. It is located in Mecca. About 2 million Muslims visit each year!

Did you know? Muslims on the hajj must follow special rules. This includes not shaving or cutting nails. They must not use perfume or cologne. Pilgrims must also wear white.

"Did you hear that man at the feast?" Father says. "His family traveled by camel!"

I feel grateful we flew here by plane.

Faiza says, "I'll bet his backside is hurting."

"Faiza!" Mother calls, but we all laugh. Hajj is an honor, but for some it's a greater sacrifice.

We pack and talk about all the great things we experienced. I feel closer to Islam and hope to come back someday. And maybe I'll travel by camel!

ACTIVITY

Henna

Yasir's cousin does henna designs on hands to celebrate. You can do these temporary designs as well.

WHAT YOU NEED:

Plastic gloves

1/8 cup (10 grams) of henna powder

1/8 cup (30 milliliter) of lemon juice

Bowl

1 teaspoon (5 mL) of sugar

1 teaspoon (5 mL) of essential oil

Plastic wrap

Spoon

Applicator bottle or plastic tubing bags

Stencil designs (optional)

INSTRUCTIONS:

1. Wear gloves. Henna is a dye power and will stain.
2. Mix the henna powder and lemon juice in a bowl.
3. Add the sugar and essential oil. Sugar helps prevent the paste from drying out. Essential oil helps the henna stain darker.
4. Cover the bowl with plastic wrap. Let it sit for at least 24 hours in a warm area.
5. After 24 hours, spoon the paste into an applicator bottle or bag.
6. Apply the design using a stencil or your imagination!
7. Let the henna sit on the skin for at least 24 hours. Avoid getting water on the design for as long as possible.

TIMELINE of MAJOR EVENTS

570: Muhammad is born in Mecca

610: Angel Jibrail visits Muhammad to impart Allah's wisdom

622: Islam is founded by Muhammad; this is also the year Muhammad went to Medina with his followers; this is also called hijrah (HEEJ-ruh)

632: Muhammad dies

750: The beginning of Islam's Golden Age

1672: The Ottoman Empire sees its height

1947: Palestine is divided, creating Israel

1969: The Organization of the Islamic Conference is created

2001: On September 11, the United States is attacked by the terrorist organization al-Qaeda

2008: Muslim and Roman Catholic leaders meet to condemn terrorism and encourage religious tolerance

LEARN MORE

FURTHER READING

Marsico, Katie. *Islam.* Ann Arbor, MI: Cherry Lake Publishing, 2017.

Raatma, Lucia. *Islam.* Mankato, MN: Compass Point Books, 2010.

Self, David. *The Lion Encyclopedia of World Religions.* Oxford, UK: Lion Children's, 2008.

WEBSITES

BBC—Ramadan: What is Ramadan?
https://www.bbc.co.uk/newsround/24566691

PBS Learning Media—The Hajj: Islamic Pilgrimage
https://dptv.pbslearningmedia.org/resource/sj14-soc-hajj/the-hajj-islamic-sacred-pilgrimage/#.WPoxjtyIqUk

GLOSSARY

caliph (KAY-luhf) an Islamic leader

descendants (dih-SEN-duhntz) people who are related to someone from the past

Eid al-Fitr (EYED-AHL-FIH-tuhr) the celebration of the end of Ramadan

hajj (HAHJ) a mandatory pilgrimage to Mecca for Muslims

halal food (huh-LAHL FOOD) food permitted by the Qur'an

icon (EYE-kahn) an important figure

imam (ih-MAHM) a Muslim leader and teacher

monotheism (mah-nuh-THEE-ih-zuhm) the belief in one God

mosque (MAHSK) an Islamic temple

polytheism (PAH-lee-thee-ih-zuhm) the belief in multiple gods

Qur'an (kuh-RAN) Islam's holy book

Shi'a (SHEE-ah) an Islamic branch, believe leadership should come from descendants of Muhammad

Sufi (SOO-fee) an Islamic branch, believe Muslims should focus on spiritual growth rather than power and wealth

Sunna (SOO-nuh) religious text that relays Muhammad's words and deeds, as well as those of his companions

Sunni (SOO-nee) the largest Islamic branch, believe their leader should be elected by Muslims

tawaf (TAH-woof) the ceremonious walking around the Ka'ba in Mecca

wudu (WOO-doo) a Muslim preparation for prayer, which includes washing faces, arms, and hands

Zakat ul-Fitr (zuh-KAT UHL-FIH-tuhr) a charitable contribution to the needy, customary before Ramadan

INDEX